TABLE

GRACES

Illustrated by Laura Cronin
Edited and introduced by D. S. Baker

Appletree Press

First published in 1995 by
The Appletree Press Ltd
19-21 Alfred Street
Belfast BT2 8DL
Tel: +44 1232 243074 Fax: +44 1232 246756

A Little Book of Table Graces

A catalogue record for this book is available in
The British Library.

ISBN 0 86281 551 7

9 8 7 6 5 4 3 2 1

INTRODUCTION

In one of the Essays of Elia, Charles Lamb offered his theory of how grace before meals began "...in the early times of the world, and the hunter-state of man, when dinners were precarious things, and a full meal was something more than a common blessing, when a belly-full was a wind-fall, and looked like a special providence. In the shouts and triumphal songs with which, after a season of sharp abstinence, a lucky booty of deer's or goat's flesh would naturally be ushered home, existed, perhaps, the germ of the modern grace."

Grace in this sense comes from the Latin *gratias* - thanks. Whatever we think of "Elia's" typically imaginative picture, there is evidence in ancient literature for thanksgiving before food. The Homeric heroes invoked the Gods as they performed sacrifice. Jews, Greeks and Romans all asked a blessing before meals. Christianity inherited the practice. Before feeding the five thousand, and at the Last Supper, Jesus blessed the bread before dividing it. In Acts, Chapter XXVII, St Paul, "took some bread, gave thanks to God in front of them all, broke it, and began to eat".

As the Lord's Prayer reminds us, God is seen as the

provider of our daily bread, and it was natural for the Christian to give thanks before eating. With the development of the monastery, when monks or nuns sat at a common table, the simple exercise became more complex, with graces that might be chanted. Into the Middle Ages and beyond, in schools, guild halls and other institutions, the practice of grace before (and after) meals developed. There were graces for special days and occasions, graces for fish-only meals. Each institution had its particular and often lengthy form. Until the sixteenth century, graces were almost always in Latin, the language of the sacraments.

From the Reformation, the domestic grace became common for family use. Woe betide the hungry child who reached for spoon or fork before grace was intoned by the senior adult present. In some families, however, it was the youngest member who recited the grace. Nowadays, the custom of grace before meals is far less common, and can cause embarrassment to those who do not expect it. We take our daily bread very much for granted. But this little collection sharpens our sense of how our ancestors felt and behaved, and may offer some new or unfamiliar graces for use today.

ANCIENT AND MEDIEVAL GRACES

S IT NOMEN *Domini benedictum*
Per Jesum Christum, Salvatorem nostrum,

Amen

May the name of the Lord be blessed
Through Jesus Christ, our Saviour,

Amen

OUR LORD God, you are the Bread that is eaten in heaven, the Bread that gives life, the Food that truly nourishes the whole world. You came down from heaven and gave life; you guide us through this present existence and you have promised that there will be another for us to enjoy after this. Bless then, our food and drink, and enable us to take them without sinning. May we receive them thankfully and give you glory for them, for it is you who confer all good gifts upon us. Blessed and glorious is your name, ever worthy of honour.

2nd century

WE GIVE Thee thanks, our Father, for the holy Resurrection which Thou hast manifested to us through Jesus, Thy Son, and even as this bread which is here upon this table was formerly scattered abroad and has been made compact, so may Thy Church be reunited from the ends of the earth for Thy Kingdom, for Thine is the power and the glory, for ever and ever.

Amen

4th century, attributed to St Athanasius, Bishop of Alexandria

Benedictus es, *Domine, qui nutris me a pueritia mea, qui das escas omni carni, imple gaudio et laetitia corda nostra, ut abundemus in omne opus bonus in Christo Jesu Domino nostro.*

You are blessed, Lord, who have fed me from my infancy, who give us all our food. Fill our hearts with joy and pleasure, that we may abound in good works in the name of Jesus Christ our Lord.

5th century

R EFICE NOS, *Domine, donis tuis, et opulentiae tuae largitate sustente. Per Jesum Christum Dominum nostrum.*

Feed us Lord, with your gifts, and sustain us with your great generosity. Through Jesus Christ our Lord.

7th century

LORD CHRIST, we pray for thy mercy on our table,
And what Thy gentle hands have give Thy men,
Let it be blessed.
All that we have came from Thy lavish heart and gentle
hand,
All that is good is Thine, for Thou art good.
And you that eat, give thanks for it to Christ,
And let the words you utter be only peace,
For Christ loved peace. He it was Who said,
Peace I give unto you; my peace I leave with you.
Grant that your own may be a generous hand
Breaking the bread for all poor men;
Sharing the food.
Christ shall receive the bread you gave His poor,
And shall not delay in giving you reward.

8th century. Alcuin of York, counsellor to Charlemagne

BLESSED YOU are, Lord;
You have fed me from my earliest days;
You give food to every living creature.
Fill our hearts with joy and delight;
Let us always have enough,
And something to spare for works of mercy,
In honour of Christ Jesus our Lord.
Through him may glory, honour and power
Be yours forever.

Amen
Greek Church. Attributed to St John Chrysostom

BENEDICTUS BENEDICAT. *Per Jesum Christum, Dominum nostrum.*

Amen

May the Blessed One bless us. Through Jesus Christ, our Lord.

Amen

SIXTEENTH AND SEVENTEENTH CENTURY GRACES

DOMINUS JESUS *sit potus et esus.*

May the Lord Jesus be drink and food.

16th century. Martin Luther

OCULI OMNIUM *spectant in Te, Deus! Tu das illis escas tempore opportune. Aperis manum Tuam et imples omne animal Tua benedictione. Mensae coelestis nos participes facias, Deus, rex aeternae gloriae.*

The eyes of all are upon Thee, O God! You provide them with their food at the right times. Open Your hand and fill every creature with Your blessing. Let us sit with You at the heavenly table, God, eternal king of glory.

Grace before meal, 16th century. Brasenose College, Oxford

Q UI NOS *creavit, redemit et pavit, sit benedictus in aeternam. Deus exaudi orationem nostram. Agimus tibi gratias, Pater coelestis, pro fundatoribus nostris; aliusque benefactoribus nostris; humiliter Te precantes ut eorum numerum benignissime adaugeas. Ecclesiam Catholicam et populum Christianum custodi. Haereses et errores omnes extirpa. Reginam nostram et subditos ejus defende. Pacem da et conserva per Christum Dominum nostrum.*

You who created, redeemed and protect us, be blessed forever. Hear our prayer, O God. We thank you, heavenly Father, for our benefactors, and humbly pray that their numbers may be increased by your generosity. Guard the Universal Church and the Christian people. Stamp out all heresy and error. Preserve our Queen and her subjects. Give us lasting peace. In the name of Christ our Lord.

Grace after meal, 16th century. Brasenose College, Oxford

THE EYES of all things do look up and trust in Thee; O Lord, thou givest them their meat in due season. Thou dost open thy hand and fillest with Thy blessing everything living. Good Lord, bless us and all Thy goods which we receive of Thy bountiful liberality: through Jesus Christ our Lord.

16th century. Attributed to Queen Elizabeth I

To GOD Who gives our daily bread
A thankful song we raise,
And pray that He Who sends us food
Ay fill our hearts with praise.

16th century. Thomas Tallis

O MOST merciful Father, who of thy gracious goodness hast heard the devout prayer of thy Church, and turned our dearth and scarcity into cheapness and plenty; We give thee humble thanks for this thy special bounty; beseeching thee to continue thy loving kindness unto us, that our land may yield us her fruits of increase, to thy glory and our comfort, through Jesus Christ our Lord.

Amen
Book of Common Prayer

I AM content with what I have,
Little it be or much;
And, Lord, contentment still I crave,
Because Thou savest such.

17th century. John Bunyan

G OD! To my little meal and oil
Add but a bit of flesh to boil
And thou my pipkinnet shalt see
Give a wave-offering to thee.

17th century. Robert Herrick

MOST GRACIOUS God, who has given us Christ and with Him all that is necessary to life and godliness; we thankfully take this our food as the gift of Thy bounty, procured by His merits. Bless it to the nourishment and strength of our frail bodies to fit us for Thy cheerful service.

17th century. Richard Baxter

FATHER, SUPPLY my every need!
Sustain the life thyself hast given;
Call for the never-failing bread
The manna that comes down from heaven.

Thy gracious fruits of righteousness,
Thy blessings unexhausted, store,
In me abundantly increase,
Nor let me ever hunger more.

Susanna Wesley

Before the meal:

BLESS US, o Lord, and these Thy gifts, which we are about to receive of Thy bounty, through Christ our Lord.

Amen

After the meal:

WE GIVE Thee thanks, Almighty God, for all thy benefits, Who livest and reignest without end.

Amen

English Catholic grace

EIGHTEENTH AND NINETEENTH CENTURY GRACES

FOR LIFE and good health,
For good company and good cheer,
May the Giver of all things
Make us thankful.

18th century

BE PRESENT at our table, Lord,
Be here and everywhere adored,
Thy creatures bless, and grant that we
May feast in Paradise with Thee.

18th century Wesleyan grace. John Cennick

THY PROVIDENCE supplies my food
And it is Thy blessing makes it good.
My soul is nourished by Thy word;
Let soul and body praise the Lord.

18th century. William Cowper

GOD HATH given us all things richly to enjoy.
Let us enjoy them.

19th century

SCOTTISH GRACES

BE WITH me, o God, at the breaking of bread,
Be with me, o God, when I have fed;
Naught come to my body my soul to pain
Naught able my contrite soul to stain.

From the Gaelic

WITHOUT THY sunshine and Thy rain,
We would not have Thy golden grain.
Without Thy love we'd not be fed:
We thank Thee for our daily bread

From the Gaelic

SOME HA'E meat, that canna eat,
And some ha'e nane, that want it.
But we ha'e meat, and we can eat,
And sae the Lord be thankit.

18th century. Robert Burns

An Irish Grace

Before the meal:

BLESS US, o Lord,
Bless our food and drink,
You Who have so dearly redeemed us
And have saved us from evil,
As You have given us this share of food,
May You give us our share of the everlasting glory.

After the meal:

PRAISE TO the King of Plenty,
Praise every time to God,
A hundred praises and thanks to Jesus Christ,
For what we have eaten and shall eat.

CHILDREN'S GRACES

THANK YOU for the world so sweet,
　Thank you for the food we eat,
Thank you for the birds that sing;
Thank you, God, for everything.

19th century. E. Rutter Leatham

HERE A little child I stand,
　Heaving up my either hand;
Cold as paddocks though they be,
Here I lift them up to Thee,
For a benison to fall,
On our meat and on us all.

17th century. Robert Herrick

IT IS very nice to think
The world is full of meat and drink
With little children saying Grace
In every Christian kind of place.

19th century. Robert Louis Stevenson

COME, LORD Jesus, be our Guest
May this food to us be bless'd.

Said by the children of Dr George Carey,
Archbishop of Canterbury

GOD IS great,
God is good
Let us thank Him for this food.

DEAR GOD,
Thank You for my home
And the rain and sun;
Thank You for my toys, and food and fun.
Thank You for my school and all Your gifts to me;
Thank You, God, for Your gifts to me;
Thank You, God, for Your generosity.

Starting the Day

THIS IS the day the Lord has made -
Give thanks for toast and marmalade.

LORD, AS we begin the day,
Help us not to be like porridge -
Stiff and stodgy, slow to stir,
But like cornflakes -
Crisp and light and ready to serve.

Lord, as we begin the day,
Help us not to be like cornflakes -
Lightweight, cold and brittle;
But like porridge -
Warm and full of goodness and comfort.

EVERYDAY GRACES

Before the meal:

FOR WHAT we are about to receive, may the Lord make us truly thankful.

Amen

After the meal:

FOR WHAT we have received, may the Lord make us truly thankful.

Amen

Before the meal:

BLESS, O Lord, these gifts to our use, and ourselves to Thy service, for Christ's sake.

Amen

After the meal:

FOR THESE and all His mercies, God's holy name be praised, for Christ's sake.

Amen

MAY GOD bless this food to our use
and ourselves in His service.
For Jesus' sake.

Amen

BLESSED ART Thou, o Lord our God, King of the
Universe, Who bringest forth bread from the earth.

A Jewish grace

FOR GOOD food, good friends and good fellowship,
We thank you, Lord, in Jesus' name.

Acknowledgments:
The graces in this little book have come from many sources. The publishers gratefully thank all those who suggested graces for inclusion. Special thanks are due to the Archbishop of Canterbury and his Chaplain, the Rev. Canon Colin Fletcher.